UNREASONABLE PRAISE

Endorsement

"Terces lets us into her inner world in a v[...]
and love for others."
-BOB GOFF AUTHOR OF 4 NEW YORK TIME[...]

"Terces not only has created food to fill the body, she now has written words to fill your soul. She candidly writes about pain, loss, and redemption in a way that will forever change you and inspire you to hope again."
-BIANCA JUAREZ OLTHOFF, PASTOR, PODCAST, AND BEST-SELLING AUTHOR OF HOW TO HAVE YOUR LIFE NOT SUCK

"This book is a work of love. Terces so generously invites us into her story while simultaneously returning us to our own, through a soulful and evocative invitation to live the truth of our own stories. Modern proverbial wisdom baked with love and light."
-ELYSE SNIPES, LMFT, FOUNDER OF RADICAL WELLNESS COLLABORATIVE

"A modern elder is someone who uses their lived wisdom as a contribution to upcoming generations, In the pages of this book Terces does exactly that."
- CHIP CONLEY, HOSPITALITY ENTREPRENEUR AND FOUNDER OF THE MODERN ELDER ACADEMY

"Through this book, you'll experience the powerful journey Terces' navigated in bringing her to who she is today. This book invites you to sit across from her at her kitchen table and enter into a conversation that slips into the night while sipping a glass of wine as you soak in every last bit of wisdom from her stories. Terces invites you into her heart through the telling of her powerful story, and in turn, invites you into your own."
-JOANNA WATERFALL, FOUNDER OF YELLOW CO

"Terces is a messenger, bringing great wisdom to the page. Unreasonably Grateful feels like reading a personal diary filled with brilliant and sincere self-realizing entries; reminding us that personal growth is ongoing - and that it's never too late to be who you are called to be: Love."
-JASON MRAZ, SINGER/SONGWRITER

Ordering Information: For information about special discounts for bulk purchases and wholesale, please contact the publisher at the website address listed above.

Edited by: Jennifer Rosenthal
Cover Photo by: Susan LeStrange

Printed by Ingram Spark (www.ingramspark.com) in the United States of America.

First Printing: 2022

ISBN 9798218061685 (Paperback)
ISBN 9798218061739 (eBook)

UNREASONABLY GRATEFUL

Living in Grace by Choice

TERCES ENGELHART

All there is
is love.

Everything else is
our resistance to it.

TABLE OF CONTENTS

FORWARD

I first met Terces on her farm. I followed her as she bounded through her day. When Terces makes bread she keeps the ingredients pure and precise kneading in love and wisdom. She writes the way she makes bread. She welcomes every soul to her table where she effortlessly feeds their souls with goodness. With this book, we feast at her table. Terces lives generous and free and only free people free other people. Hers is the "beauty of a shared life."

Terces can do anything. Whether the currents are for or against her, she refuses to give up.

Swim in any direction Terces and we follow you because LOVE drives you forward. Thank you for sharing your life with us.

Kim McManus
Mosaic, MOSAIC GLOBAL, Director

INTRODUCTION
Truth and Lies

I was born Marsha Faye Lane, the third daughter in a military family. My father, a Navy Commander, was a sea plane (PBY Catalina) pilot during WWII, my mother taught Home Economics until she had her first child. We moved often and I learned to make friends quickly. I also learned to let go of friendships when we moved. However, I often hoped I would see those friends again.

Raised as a competitive swimmer who stopped eating to reach a weight goal, set by a coach. Sexually abused by a physician at 16 and kept it a secret for 20 years while struggling with an eating disorder.

Growing up in a Christian home I had my first personal encounter with Jesus as I lay in a hospital bed no longer wanting to live.

As a friend and pastor told me years later, I was literally "born again."

My spiritual path was messy and my recovery took years, guided by an internal voice, full of wisdom and unconditional love. Now 36 years later, I am still growing.

An entrepreneur at heart, I am passionate about the possibility of business as a means to do good in this world.

My plant based restaurants, Cafe Gratitude and Gracias Madre, were created as a way to encourage and support the transformation of others and to spread the practice of gratitude. Something I believe gives us access to the possibility of a loving Father.

I'm the mother of three and married to a man who has two children. Together our five children have blessed us with 15 grandchildren.

Today, I live on a farm with my husband and invite people to come, slow down, and draw closer to nature.

I have written for years, but it is not until now that I have been able to finish what I started, and let go. This book is my let go.

Ever since my journey brought me to freedom, I've known I would write this book, it was just a matter of when. I suspect anytime one of us gets free we want to set others free as well, freedom is like that, it is meant to be shared with the world.
The abuse I kept a secret for twenty years was my trap and only in my becoming transparent was I able to experience the freedom that awaited me.

I had to get beyond thinking I could free someone else and instead simply share my journey and trust that there are those who are ready to hear, and some ready to act. You know who you are.

For over three decades I have been recovering the broken off pieces of myself, and now it is time to surrender those pieces to you.

Each story is a seed I have scattered throughout these pages. Sit with each one, let it rest in your mind and heart, toss it around, wrestle with it if necessary, some will take root, tend to those and let them grow.

The only impossible journey is the one you never start.

CHAPTER ONE
My Invitation

My Invitation

Dear Lord
  a tired child am I
  Now within my bed, I lie
  Send the angels watch to keep
  Close beside me while I sleep
  All the wrong I've done today
  Loving Father wash away
  Help me as I older grow
  More and more I'd love to know
  God Bless
  Everyone all over the world,
  Amen

The time between me reciting that prayer nightly and now is my life. It has been filled with memories both precious and painful, all of them jewels that shine in their own unique way. As the light shines through them, they come alive. They are in no particular order, other than the one I put them in, for no particular reason that I can think of now.

It took a while for some to shine, or even for the light to pass through them. Like mine, you have yours. It's my prayer that perhaps as you read my memories the light will shine through yours as well. Sometimes it's easier that way, at least I can see the light in others before I see it in myself. I guess that's why we need one another, to shine the light of love.

The only real invitation is, who I am is love and I am here to serve you.

CHAPTER TWO (1986-89)
The Four Guides

Over the first several years of my recovery, I would be given a guide, one at a time, and I made that guide the focus of my life. Each has been a powerful teacher and has continued to guide me all these years later. Whenever I feel off-balance, out of sync, or somehow distracted, I go back through these and usually I discover someplace in my life where I am not being fully honest. It is always a good starting point for me. That might be with me, with others, or simply not speaking up at all. While they all work together I have shared them in the order they were given to me. They are woven throughout the stories I have shared.

1. Tell the truth
2. Stay in the moment
3. Face your fears
4. Open up to love

Freedom is impossible without faith in free people.

CHAPTER THREE (1967)
You Matter

I was lying in a military hospital bed with an IV, I was 17 years old, 5'8" and weighed 90 pounds. My body was swollen with liquid. My mother, bless her heart, was bringing in cheese curls and Mountain Dew just wanting me to start eating and gain weight so life could go back to normal. I wanted the world to go away and leave me alone.

I had a dream that night, where I seemed to be above myself looking down at my body lying there when I heard a voice speaking to me. I can't tell you how but I knew that voice as Jesus, I just knew. He spoke softly with such kindness saying he wanted me to go back and stay, I asked him why? He said, "for the others, to help them."

I'm not sure why that made such a difference for me, but it did. Perhaps it was simply not thinking about myself, my own struggles, and shifting my attention to being of some use to someone else. Maybe it was just feeling like "someone" was on my side, knew what I was going through, and wanted me to stay. Whatever it was, I started fighting for my life. I felt as if I had a purpose now that was bigger than my pain.

Getting out of the hospital was my first step. I didn't do it in necessarily the most honorable way. I began to drink copious amounts of water before weigh-in each day, hoping to gain enough weight to be discharged. I would look for any heavy objects to put in my robe pockets, anything to tip the scales on my behalf. It was for a higher purpose.

My story is being birthed from the words I took to heart that day..
"Go back and stay...for the others to help them."

I have learned that helping is actually a mutually beneficial experience, I don't have anyone's answers, and they don't necessarily need me, we are simply traveling this road together and our stories bind us in a way that loses us as well. That is the beauty of this shared life we all live.

If you struggle with believing in Jesus, or a loving God, so have I, welcome home. When I mention either of them see if you can identify just what it is that comes up for you, there may be some healing wanting to take place in that area. I actually think the struggle is part of what it takes to discover just how loved we are. I am no Bible scholar but I know the stories in that ancient book are filled with people struggling.

I've often said the unceasing flow of everything that is in, through, and around us all the time is a lot to be with. So we have a sieve in place that only allows a certain amount in, the amount we can personally handle. I have learned that I can only enlarge the holes in my sieve as I let go of it being personal. Part of identifying where I am blocked allows me to then consciously choose to keep that block in place or let go.

Usually, when it feels like too much for me, there is something for me to consider letting go of so more love can flow through. Consider that God's ways are the ways in which love awakens us. As you and I mature on the spiritual path we will consider ourselves blessed and fortunate by all the ways in which we never cease to be delighted by God.

Look for a silver lining in the darkest of clouds.

CHAPTER FOUR (1967)
No One Would Believe Me

I kept trying to remember to say, PLEASE. My mind was foggy, my body numb, thoughts just swirled around making no sense at all, I didn't seem to be able to take hold of anything. Stop, PLEASE stop, PLEASE don't do that, was all I could mutter as tears streamed from my eyes and down my cheeks, my throat closing, and my words muffled. My doctor stepped back, walked over to the sink, and washed his hands as he said, "Don't tell anyone, they won't believe you anyway." "I have a family, and your family already didn't believe you so what makes you think they will believe you now?" I didn't answer, laying there like a stunned bird who had just force-fully slammed against a clean window, too clean to see that it was even there. The innocence of my vision was crashing in on me as I lay still. He went on, "Remember you asked for it, even said it was okay that I didn't call the nurse in." "I'm finished with you now, get up, get dressed and I don't need to see you again." "You are free to go."

I sat up, the tears now rolled down my cheeks, I pulled the sheet up over myself as he walked out of the room and closed the door behind him. I sat silently. I still could not seem to think, my thoughts floated by without sticking. I was nauseous.

I started putting on my clothes. I could barely breathe. No sooner had my lungs filled with air when they seemed to
deflate before I exhaled, never seeming to fill up enough to slow my heart-beat and calm myself down. I gasped for more air as I sobbed.

I HAD said it was okay to not call in the "too busy" nurse, as he had put it.

I HAD thought of how proud he would be of the progression I was making to gain even a little weight, after being hospitalized for anorexia.

I HAD wanted him to be pleased with me.

My parents HADN'T believed me when he told them, after being taken in for a consultation by my mother because my periods had stopped, that I was probably pregnant and the parents are always the last to know in cases like this.

I WAS a case.

The urine sample HAD come back positive causing me to even doubt myself.

I HAD begun to think perhaps it was the second coming of Jesus, as I didn't even have a boyfriend.

I felt crazy.

My parents HAD taken me out of school, not wanting to shame the family, and kept me home until my examination appointment. I was NOT pregnant and I HAD NOT been believed.

My parents HAD lied about what was going on, to avoid being embarrassed by me.

HE WAS RIGHT was my conclusion to this merry-go-round of thoughts.

NO ONE WOULD BELIEVE ME.

I only think we see the before in a life when the after has already taken place.

CHAPTER FIVE (1986)
A Crack in the Facade

I was in the bathroom one morning after probably finishing all the toast I had made for the kids along with any leftover breakfast from their plates. When I walked out after throwing it all up my daughter was there sitting on the floor. She looked up at me asking, "Mommy are you ok?" I shrugged her question off with an aloof, "Of course I am." When suddenly I saw a brief flash of light out of the corner of my eye and the awareness came flooding in, that I was doing to her exactly what was done to me, teaching her to mistrust herself. I can't say exactly how it all happened in what seemed like a second but there was an opening, a crack in my facade, I felt a warm presence deep inside myself. I hugged my daughter and told her I loved her before going upstairs to get dressed. While showering I heard a voice, a voice I knew, say "tell the truth." I thought to myself, I always tell the truth. The phone rang, I jumped out of the shower, with a towel wrapped around me, as I heard my own voice respond to the question of where their package was, " I mailed it yesterday," while looking at it sitting on my desk right in front of me. My lie got my attention.

No sooner had I dressed and got the kids in the car when I heard another lie and then another came out of my mouth. I was speechless.

I sat in the school parking lot for several minutes as lies began to flood my mind, one after another. I lied all the time. Along with the paralyzing conviction of my lying came a small opening as an invitation to start being truthful.

I discovered most of my life was a lie, I wasn't living, I was acting.

Light will flow in through the smallest of cracks, watch for it, it is there. See if you can catch a glimpse of it.

19

CHAPTER SIX (1966)

Five Pounds

Our swim coach decided we should all weigh the same, attempting to have us look more like one person instead of a team of eight synchronized swimmers. We were competing on a national level and the stakes were high. She announced the target weight.

Always wanting to please, I cut back on what I was eating and started weighing myself daily, while still swimming four to six hours a day.

I was living in a friend's home with my father while he was getting his teaching credential after retiring from 20 plus years as a Naval pilot. My mother still lived in our family home in Carmel Valley. No one was really paying attention to my meals. I weighed the same day after day, so I cut back even more.

I arrived at the pool, was weighed before working out, and still no change. One day she said, "You aren't trying."

I dove in to start my mile of laps and felt hot with anger. My mind replayed the same tape over and over, "How dare she say I'm not trying I'll show her, I'll show her, I'll show her," as I pushed off against the wall on each turn.

I quit eating.

I would suck on ice cubes and eat lettuce.
As I stepped on the scale after a few days, I noticed I was now losing a pound a day.

I was elated.

I hit the target weight. I could hardly wait to get to the pool and "show her". I could only imagine how proud of me she would be.

I stepped on the scale, the needle balanced on my target, she looked down and recorded the number, she looked up at me and then said, "Too thin, gain five."

That was it.

I dove in to start my workout as tears poured out, mixing with the pool water as I dug another stroke into the cool water. I could feel the warmth of the tears on my face. I remember thinking, whatever I was feeling must be hatred, I had never felt it before.

So simple are the words, gain five. I wish it had been that easy.
 I couldn't start eating again, I didn't know why. I was filled with fear.
 I was cooking for my father and feeding him seemed to satisfy me.
 I wasn't hungry.
 I was numb.

Let someone into your angry feelings, don't hold them in, let them out.

CHAPTER SEVEN (1950-1960)

Just Say NO!

I've often thought if only I could have said, no.
As a child growing up we weren't allowed to say no to an adult or anyone in an authority position. It always had to be "Yes."

Yes, I'll set the table.
Yes, I can help my sister.
Yes, I won't tell anyone.
Yes, I don't mind
Yes, you don't have to call the nurse in.

If we did say no, we had our mouths washed out with soap.
I remember trying to pretend that I liked the taste of soap.

Have your no's be a yes to you.

CHAPTER EIGHT (2019)
Truth and Lies

Going back over my past feels a bit crazy for sure. I find myself wanting to apologize again to the people in my life who went through all those years with me. I am certainly grateful for where I am and I am trusting my story will make a difference for others. I apologize for any pain, loss, or heart-break that I caused. You are dear to me, all of you and you know who you are.

When what I was raised to believe came crashing down I felt direction-less. Prematurely out on my own with no GPS. I don't think my parents intended it to be this way, they may not have even known. I certainly wasn't sharing.

Looking back it's not hard to see how I missed so many opportunities. I lived a lie.

Recently I felt as if God was doing surgery on my heart, swiftly cutting away lies from the truth of my life. I hesitated, I started arguing for the lies wondering if there was truth in them when God spoke to me saying, "There is no truth in a lie, let it go." I wanted it to be that easy, perhaps it is, stop thinking about it.

The renewal of the mind, stop thinking about it.

We come to believe that lies are true, remember there is no truth in a lie.

CHAPTER NINE (2019)
A Wounded Harbor

I find myself wondering where it all began. I'm not sure it even matters. It seems more like a collection of small, insignificant events that eventually added up.

I found an uncanny comfort in my ex-husband sharing with me, not all that long ago, that when a young girl is sexually abused it's an assault on God, it disrupts a primary relationship that is intended to keep one safe, a fatally wounded harbor.

We are created for a trusting union, when that doesn't happen there is core mistrust that weaves its way into every area of life. "I'm broken", "I'm alone", "I'm ruined", "I'm used," are all expressions of it. A suit of armor is adorned to protect, however, it also keeps you separate, shut out, locked in.

Reading recently about why abused women often return to their abuser, I was struck by the truth of living in what is known, how facing it brings it to the surface, and makes it real. Not facing it keeps it hidden and in a way you are safe, in a protective cocoon. Staying with what we can handle, what we can control, somehow seems safer than facing the unknown of the truth.

I often had a reoccurring dream where I was being buried alive yet when I went to call out I didn't have a voice, I wasn't able to make a sound.

I'm still asking myself if the comfort I feel now is simply relief from all the years of guilt and shame or is it that I now know the wounding wasn't fatal, and that feels so good, good enough to want freedom for others.

You are seen, you are heard, and you are valued.

CHAPTER TEN (1960)

What do you want to be when you grow up?

I grew up wanting to be a trapeze artist in a circus. Flying through the air and trusting I would be caught before I fell seemed exciting.

While I never joined the circus, there have been so many times when I realize I lived at risk and yet was somehow protected, cared for, and caught by grace.

Let your outer desires give you clues to your inner world.

CHAPTER ELEVEN (1993)

Katharine Hepburn

I felt as if I was in a new world. One I often felt lost in. A mother of three, in my late thirties, and yet unsure of just about everything.

I had always admired and been inspired by Katharine Hepburn. I saw a picture of her on the cover of People magazine at a check-out stand and thought, she won't live forever, I should write to her and share how much I appreciate her, how she inspires me. As I walked to my car I realized I was beginning to feel after years of being numb.

I sat down to write and couldn't even figure out how to start.... was it, Dear Ms. Hepburn, or Hey Katherine.... as silly as it seems is how silly I felt. I crossed it out and tossed the paper into the basket. I did this more than once.

The letter was always on my mind. While in a bookstore one day I picked up a copy of her autobiography and ran my finger down page after page, drinking in every word as if I was searching for something. I came across the address of her family summer home in Connecticut.

I felt like a teenager who was star-struck, living in a middle-aged body.

I finally crafted a letter of gratitude and shared a bit of the struggle I was going through in recovery.

I walked past a mailbox on the street a day or so later and while I was still hesitant to drop the letter in, I just knew there was a lesson in this for me, so I let it slip out of my fingers and fall to the pile of other letters awaiting pickup.

I immediately wished I could retrieve it.

Months later there was a small envelope with a handwritten New York return address that arrived in my mail. To my surprise, I opened it and found a sweet handwritten note from Katharine Hepburn thanking me for writing to her and encouraging me in my own life. I looked at the shaky handwriting and could almost hear her voice. I thought about her taking the time to write a handwritten reply. I felt gratitude seeping into the cracks in my heart.

Don't wait to do what calls to you, even if you feel foolish.

CHAPTER TWELVE (1990)
Uncanny Guidance

I continued to be guided and I listened. I also obeyed.

I started brushing my teeth and my hair, holding the brush with my non-dominant hand. It sounds so simple and yet it kept me present, alert, out of my habitual ways.

I drove different routes to wherever I was going, sometimes letting myself experience the feeling of being lost or out of control. It felt good to just let go and trust in this small way.

I spent at least a year saying, "I don't know" to almost every question that was asked of me. I was so used to having quick responses, even if I didn't really know the answer. I just made up something, in other words, I lied. The space that was created in "not knowing" allowed me to slow down and take deeper breaths. I also began to discover more about others and myself.

I discovered I didn't know when I was hungry or full. It was uncanny, even scary. So I waited, usually having a glass of water and sitting still, slowing my world down a bit.

I started looking at menus when dining out and asking myself, "what do I want?" Focusing on where the wanting was coming from and how discon-nected I felt from those wants sometimes. I was afraid to want, in my world I had it connected to being selfish.
I can still recall the day I realized that what I actually wanted was good for me. I wept.

Whenever I would recognize the distraction or old ways sneaking in I did something simple, I sat down. It didn't matter where I was. It could be the middle of the street or an aisle in the grocery market. Sitting down would disrupt the old pathway and usher me into the present moment. It worked, giving me the time I needed to be attentive. Fortunately, my children thought this was fun, and their acceptance and freedom freed me. We laughed together.

You can create new
practices that
support your
healing.

Terces

One day I pulled our car into the parking lot of Blockbuster and told the kids, "I'm going to change my name." They were excited, and started suggesting names they liked. "How about Nicole, or Ashley?" I shared with them that "God gave me a new name, it's Terces." They were still for a bit and then suggested, "What about Julie?" We went inside and picked out a movie and on the way home I told them the meaning behind my name. "The name Terces is a reminder to not keep any secrets, to be honest, and open. If you spell Terces backward it spells Secret. God has asked me to tell the truth about my past, to not keep it a secret any longer, to be willing to be transparent".

Changing my name was challenging for me., I didn't know anyone who had changed their name and I knew my parents would be upset with me, after all, they were the ones who had named me Marsha. My children were encouraging, always cheering me on, standing by my side, and loving me.

I've been Terces for 36 years now and rarely a day goes by that someone doesn't ask me about my name or comment on it. While I certainly didn't see it, changing my name became one of the most powerful things I have ever done. It is a constant reminder to be truthful and to trust. I think God has a name for all of us that undoes our past and pulls us towards his love.

> Sometimes what we are guided to do is more powerful than we can imagine. Trust your inner guidance.

CHAPTER FOURTEEN (1991)

My Body

Getting back into trusting my own body led me to massage school. Learning healthy touch and boundaries was an important part of my healing as mine were so blurred, like lines that had been erased. I can still remember the smell of peppermint soap in the massage school shower. It was my first experience of something from a natural food store. I started wondering about all the other stores, noticing how many unnatural ones there were in comparison.

Looking for that soap I wandered into the food co-op for my first time. It was a whole new world. I felt lost and confused. I walked up and down the narrow aisles trying to find my way. Nothing looked or smelled familiar. These certainly weren't the brands my mom had clipped coupons for. The packages were smaller and there were fewer of each item on the shelf. My journey of quality over quantity began that day. The unfamiliar was my newfound friend.

Let yourself embrace the uncomfortable, the new, and the unfamiliar, be curious.

CHAPTER FIFTEEN (1966-1986)

Trapped

Food ran my life.

I had recurring nightmares of frantically looking for an empty bathroom, which was always a trek away, only to discover a long line. Or the party, holiday, or special family meal that brought up terror presenting me with either how to avoid it, or secretly eat a small family's share and then throw it up.

As a flight attendant working the galley, if I ate a cookie off of one tray I HAD to eat a cookie off of EVERY tray.

Working on Cannery Row in a Mexican restaurant I would put pieces of butter between two warm tortilla chips as I set up for opening.

When taking inventory in the hospital kitchen where I worked, I would eat my way through the packets of cookies I was counting, unable to stop.

Whether I went to a gathering or not depended on what food was being offered and how safe it would be to either binge or starve myself.

In high school I would chew on sugar coated gum balls, living on the sweetness of the syrup.

Pregnancy looked like taking a prenatal vitamin with a glass of milk just before going to sleep so that I could keep it down, while praying for a healthy baby. These shenanigans hid the real demons and kept me preoccupied. There was no escape.

Attention is our worship power, what we are attending to is what we are worshiping. We have free will, we can shift our attention.

CHAPTER SIXTEEN (1970-1990)
Mean Words

I'm sure kind things were said to me yet I recall the ones that hurt the most. " I don't love you anymore." "If I could have it my way, I would never see you again." My heart was hard and I took those in stride. It isn't any wonder looking back and pulling apart the pieces of my life's puzzle, I didn't trust myself or anyone else, I just acted as I did.

It is so much easier to focus on the negative, the painful, and the hurtful, it is powerful to practice keeping our attention on the kind, the friendly, and the loving.

CHAPTER SEVENTEEN (1993)
Jesus and the Messenger

No matter where I was I kept running into Jesus. I was on a "vision quest" in Arizona. It was pitch black on a warm desert night. I had fasted for a few days and there I sat hypersensitive to the sounds around me, looking up at the star-laden sky. I'm not sure what I was expecting but my eyes were wide and I kept lifting my eyebrows as if to open them even more hoping to be able to see something, anything. I caught my mind imagining what kind of animals might be lurking. I realized how unprepared I was. No flashlight, no phone, no blanket, just me and the desert. Afraid to sleep and not tired, just wanting something to happen, some clarity so I could call it quits. Time lingered. I must have drifted off when suddenly I heard Jesus say, "I want you to be a messenger." Startled, I replied, "I don't want to be a messenger." "Why not?" he rallied. "Because people don't want to listen." "Oh," he said with a light chuckle, "Being a messenger doesn't have anything to do with whether people listen or not." That was it. It was a moment before I realized I had my "vision." My quest was over.

Let your light shine.

CHAPTER EIGHTEEN (2020)

Catching My Breath

I had just seen the movie A Star Is Born. Shortly after, I found myself sitting at my desk clicking on all the links with Lady Gaga I could find. There was just something about her that kept me searching for more. Then I clicked on an interview with Stephen Colbert and there it was. She shared about her own sexual assault and her thoughts on Dr. Ford's testimony during the Kavanaugh hearings. I have been piecing together bits of my life and I keep finding clues that lead to the next piece in the most surprising places. Another one was found here, I read how the victims of sexual assault forget, they hide it away, and then one day when something triggers it, the box is opened and it all comes bursting forth.

I remembered when my husband, who I was separated from, had a punctured lung. He was in the hospital and I went to visit him. I brought the book, A Road Less Traveled, to give him. I really wanted to find a way to connect. My dishonest and thoughtless past had hurt him. I had no idea how to make amends. As I drove through the sentry gate to the military hospital I suddenly felt like I was having a heart attack. My chest ached, my breath tightened, and all I could do was pull over. I put my head on the steering wheel and tapped my heart with my right hand trying to breathe. When I lifted my head after a few moments I found myself looking at the building where I had been hospitalized years before. Images flashed before my mind like a slideshow. I tried to keep up with the display. I began crying. I started the car and pulled into the parking lot and waited a while.

I walked into his room, he was sitting up in bed. His eyes were cold and angry when he saw me. I didn't blame him. When he asked me what I wanted, I simply handed him the book and left. I didn't know what to say. My heart ached.

> Wounds are often buried deep inside ourselves, breathe when they arise.

CHAPTER NINETEEN (1968)

Mysteries

One of the memories that sticks with me the most when I remember my time in the military hospital is of a civilian man in a poncho coming in to see me. He shared that he was a psychologist or psychiatrist. I didn't know the difference and can't remember anyway. He asked me questions about my life. He seemed genuinely interested and was warm and kind to me. I liked him and hoped I'd see him again. He never came back and no one ever mentioned him.

Some people come into our lives briefly and yet, we are never the same again.

CHAPTER TWENTY (2018)
Validation

My high school years were split between two schools due to my swimming. I hadn't seen or kept in touch with anyone since our graduation 50 years earlier.

She gasped, as I walked up to her at our reunion picnic, "I thought you were dead!" she said. We hugged, making up for all the years in between. We had spent hours and hours at the pool together working out, she working on speed (she went on to become a Gold Medal Olympian), and I on grace, strength, and synchronization.

It was rewarding to have memories confirmed and to listen to another perspective of those early days of my weight loss. I felt faultless as someone besides myself acknowledged that Anorexia wasn't well known nor was what to do about it. My friends had felt helpless. Dealing with their own adolescent challenges was enough, let alone facing someone they cared for as I began to shrink and disappear. We laughed, we cried, we forgave, and most of all we loved and appreciated one another and our lives now.

Then something so unexpected happened. I brought up the name of our Civics teacher, whom my mother had arranged to help me pass Civics, so I could graduate, after missing so much school while hospitalized. Even in my misty memory I can still feel my paralysis when he would put his hand up my dress while my mother was getting him coffee and cookies, as we sat next to each other on the back porch, studying. My friends shared that some women had come forward just a few years ago and told about their abuse experiences when he was up for being recognized for his contribution after 50 years of being on staff. The statue they were going to erect in his honor never happened, the award was never given. The statute of limitations had passed so no legal actions were taken. I felt my lungs expand as if to take their first full breath in a long time. My body felt lighter and my mind quieter. As my shoulders relaxed I shared that I, too, had been one of those students. My friends looked at me with a mixture of sadness, love, and kindness as my fossilized doubt began melting away. Never before had I experienced any of my abuse being validated. I realized I was in the midst of an unexpected blessing and I could feel joy bubbling up inside of me.

What would you love
to have validated?

Another Version

When I picked up the phone and she said who she was, my heart raced and my throat tightened. She started speaking as if I needed a reminder of our past. When she began to say things that conflicted with my own experience I found myself resisting, then I heard the familiar inner voice say, "just listen". I quieted my reaction and sat still with my phone pressed against my ear. At one point I replied, "I am hearing what you are saying, it just doesn't match my memory." She went on, and after a while of catching me up on her life and the events that clearly led up to her finding and calling me I began to notice several inconsistencies.

Her husband and she had been the managers of the apartment building my husband and I had moved into while we were in college together. They had two small children whom I babysat and adored. I was close to them all, we often shared meals together. They were mentors to us. As she reminded me, she had taught me to drive a stick shift (which wasn't actually true as I was already driving one). One day her husband asked me to meet him at his place of work as he wanted to talk to me about something personal. I drove out to where he told me to and we sat in the park on the edge of the campus of his employer. He suddenly forced me into a sexual situation. Her story however had me forcing him. I struggled to not defend myself, "just listen," my inner voice said again. It was then I felt my heart start to melt and flood with compassion for this woman. She was trying to make sense of her life, her marriage, the insights she was having, recalling seeing gifts her husband had given her, in other women's homes. The calls continued throughout the next couple of weeks. She shared how her daughters never talked with her and then one day her youngest drew a picture of herself with her father and another woman. She discovered they were always told not to say anything to her. She was piecing her life together, feeling too late to change anything, and enough love to stick it out while still making sense of all the lies she had lived with. Each time I would hear her searching, looking for something, unsure of what it was I kept listening even though I often didn't feel like accepting the call. One day she said to me, "Somehow I knew you would be kind to me." I wanted her to find peace more than my need to have her agree with my experience with her husband. The last time we talked my familiar inner voice told me to tell her that God loves her. I did, it was silent for a moment, and then she asked if I would be willing to meet with her, I said I would. I haven't heard from her since. I pray that somehow in listening she felt loved and heard the truth.

Our pain is often intertwined with someone else's, unraveling them will reveal more of the truth.

Hide and Seek

My father was a wise and patient man. He was quiet and inward. My mother was loud and a strong force, she needed to be. I grew up trying to gain my father's attention. I wanted to know I was loved by him. In church I learned of a stern Father who judged my ways when I fell short. I wanted to earn his love also. I wanted to please my fathers.

I wanted to please my teachers.

I wanted to please my coaches.

When my efforts to attract a man's attention led to abuse over and over again my protection became an armor of numbness in which I battled with feeling anything other than ruined. I lived between a hunger to be set free and the fear of being consumed. Like a childhood game of hide and seek, I hid but so wanted to be found. Empty on the inside pretending to be full.

Addiction is all-consuming, selfish, and destructive; it eats up the person and those around it.

You are already loved.

CHAPTER TWENTY THREE (1998)
Slowing Down

I was driving along the freeway, traffic moving quickly in both directions when I suddenly had a thought. "What if there was nowhere to get to, and nothing to prove?" How different life would be. I seemed to be in such a hurry, always running behind, trying to make it … arrive on time, somewhere.

What if we have it all backward, trying so hard to do something rather than focus on who we are being?

What difference would it make if you had nothing to prove and nowhere to get to?

CHAPTER TWENTY FOUR (1990s)

Open Up To Love

When people ask me when I became a Christian, I say, I was always a Christian, I just wasn't a very good one. Today I realize it's a process, forgiveness goes deeper over time. It was one thing for me to say Jesus loves me, it was something else to really let it in. As I was guided through my recovery, the fourth message I heard was "Open up to love." Sounds pretty basic, yet for me, it was anything but simple. Over the years I have learned that when love comes in, everything that isn't love needs to get out of the way. You can't let the light in without illuminating the darkness. I suspect each of us has our own version of darkness, mine was filled with all kinds of lies. Trouble was I hadn't distinguished them as lies yet. My default is to think other people know better than I do. I guess you could call that low self-worth, but it lived for me more like I just couldn't trust myself. It wasn't that I trusted them either, I just thought they knew more.

When you say you are a Christian, you are saying that you are extravagantly loved.

Losing Myself

As we grew older I would beg my middle sister to read to me. It usually required that I sneak into the kitchen and get her a bowl of ice cream with chocolate sauce and maraschino cherries. It was no small task but so worth it to have her fill me in on Nancy Drew's latest escapades, as I would rest my head in her lap as she read.

My sister and I swam a duet routine. She was more elegant than me. She also hated competition and was always nervous and nauseous before competing.

My job was to keep an eye on her and if she messed up or forgot something I was to mess up and forget it too.

It has taken a lifetime for me to learn to just be me.

You are you, no one else. Just be you.

CHAPTER TWENTY SIX (1966-1986)
Survival

In the years of addiction, my daily life felt like a battlefield. I never felt safe. I learned to watch for clues, manipulate the other players, and numb myself to the impact of it all. That is how I survived.

I can say this now, years later, it wasn't a conscious choice then, more automatic. A learned survival tactic that I was proud to be good at. I held people at bay on the inside while appearing friendly on the outside. Covert rejection. Alone, lost, and afraid.

Slow down,
breathe, be still.

CHAPTER TWENTY SEVEN (1992-93)
Getting Rid of Stuff

Once again the familiar voice spoke, I questioned it, give away everything? Is that really what I heard? I was wanting to simplify. I did feel burdened by a house full of stuff, albeit, some good stuff too. I talked it over with my kids, told them to put away whatever they wanted to keep. My mom wanted back some of the things she had given me over the years until this ridiculous phase, as she named it, of my recovery had passed.

I purchased an old RV and put what we might need on the road into it, and then I contacted the local paper and said I was opening up our home and people could come to help themselves to whatever they wanted, FREE.

We sat in our driveway as people came and went. Walking out with their treasures in their arms some kept asking if it was really ok to go back for more. I think they were wondering what the gimmick was, struggling to trust it.

It was so freeing to just let go. I realized the memories would always be mine, and I didn't need to hold on to the things I had collected over the years. My antique blue Mason jars were being replaced with zip lock bags. My mother, who washed her plastic bags and proudly claimed what a waste of money it was to ever buy some, left me feeling as if I'd made a luxury purchase.

My eldest son wanted to stay and finish high school living with his friends across the street.

My youngest son was living with his father.

My daughter was going with me.

I remember once the house was empty, cleaned, and the keys turned in, I drove the RV downtown and parked it. I jumped in the shower and suddenly had the awareness that here I was taking a shower in the middle of the street and as the water ran down my body I giggled. I could never have imagined this.

Was it crazy? It was. I was taking off simply trusting God as we ventured out to speak with others about sexual abuse and eating disorders. The tank was full, and I had $20 dollars to my name.

We ended up stopping at some friends and I met a young man who shared he was struggling with an eating disorder. He offered to pay for gas to Santa Monica if I would take him there and share how I recovered along the way.

I'm not saying the trip was easy, there were plenty of challenges. I spoke at churches and schools, and my daughter and I had started writing inspirational sayings and putting them in packets of flower seeds and selling them along the way.

While staying with friends outside Denver, my daughter went with her friend and her two younger brothers to watch a game when they were hit by a drunk driver. My daughter was ejected from the car before it went down a ravine and stopped. The girls were the most injured and taken to the hospital. I received the call from the paramedics and called out to God for help as I drove to meet them.

My daughter broke her pelvis and ribs, and her friend shattered her ankle and had a broken hip as well. A woman who had seen the accident said something came flying out of the car and went sliding down the wet road. She didn't recognize it as a person until it came to a stop near a curb. Miraculously the window my daughter went through had broken on impact and the water from a light rain on the street had protected her from serious cuts and scrapes. We stayed in Denver until the girls had been released and they were on crutches. The settlement from that accident paid for my daughter's college tuition.

You may not know how it will all turn out, simply take the next step, let go, trust and listen.

CHAPTER TWENTY EIGHT (1990)

Psychiatric Solutions

It had been recommended that I see a Psychiatrist when my marriage began to crumble. Truth is what was actually happening were the lies I had lived with for so long we were being exposed, which was a good thing, but the truth of those lies was shattering false images. Believing things were my fault, therapy seemed like a good idea. While my lack of self-confidence didn't show as I hid behind false defiance, it was always there, second-guessing me.

The Psychiatrist spoke with me for a brief while, asking about my ability to be employed, pay my bills and follow suit. I don't think I fared so well. He recommended anti-depressants. I asked him "why?" He indicated that if I wanted to stay married he would suggest I follow his recommendation. I remember thinking, I'm not sure staying married is what's best if I have to take anti-depressants. I took the prescription and never filled it.

Make your life about what is important to YOU.

CHAPTER TWENTY NINE (1989)
Out Of Control

When I started getting stronger and my mind clearer I began pursuing support from other sources. While I continued to follow the guidance I was being given, telling the truth turned out to be confronting as well as freeing. I had been lying to myself and others for so long that there was a mess to unravel. The truth was painful since people had believed my lies. When I began to share the truth they couldn't help but question why they should believe me now. I didn't have the answer to their question, and even that felt freeing. I was discovering a newfound strength as I emerged from hiding. Transparency.

I was introduced to a woman who was a Ph.D. and had worked with women dealing with sexual trauma as well as addiction. I began to meet with her. Having kept the abuse a secret for so long it was healing to share it openly. I melted in the warmth and kindness of her ways, something I associated with someone being loving and accepting rather than critical and judgmental, something I was working on transforming in my own life. Having lived for so many years in the contradiction of who I was and who I wanted to be left me feeling evil. I had no experience of freedom from the grips of who I had become. I felt guilty most of the time.

For twenty years I was unable to eat and unable to keep down whatever I did eat. I didn't trust myself or anyone else.

My therapist worked with plant medicines. When she introduced the idea to me I hesitated. I was afraid of working with anything that felt like I would be "out of control". I had to laugh at myself when I realized how "out of control" my life was. Illusions are powerful and convincing.

When food is your drug of choice you don't have to steal or break any laws. However, I can remember pulling out of a fast-food drive-through, in a stupor, wondering how many accidents or even deaths are actually caused by someone eating while driving, only to be published as a "loss of control" of their vehicle, not their life?

Oftentimes what
we are trying to
control is actually
controlling us.

CHAPTER THIRTY (1991)
Chocolate Chip Cookies

I was driving down Highway 9 near Santa Cruz, on my way home from massage school. The window of my car was down and the wind was blowing through my hair when suddenly I had the motivation to go home and make chocolate chip cookies for my children. I could feel a prison door opening and light flooding in. I was both peaceful and excited. Somehow I knew in advance that I could bake without being trapped by past behaviors. Cookies and most sweets had been a booby trap for me in the past. I would either eat most of the dough or most of the cookies and always be left feeling defeated and guilty, hiding my shame. I have experienced this lesson over and over again. I often ask myself, "Am I ready to walk into this situation, that I wasn't able to handle powerfully in the past, only this time emerge victoriously?" The question has me slow down, check in, look at what I need to be supported (pray, reach out to a friend, breathe), keep my heart open, and then act, trusting the outcome no matter what.

What past can you reenter and this time emerge victoriously?

CHAPTER THIRTY ONE (1994)

Alcatraz

I stood at the water's edge early one December morning in my 44th year of life. It was dark and cold. I wore a thermal cap and swimsuit. I had asked a friend to pilot my swim out of the aquatic park, around Alcatraz, and back in. As I stroked through the icy water, my body slowly going numb, I passed the breakwater and kept going. My thoughts were on the rhythm of each stroke and how small I was in the vastness of the Bay. Years earlier, the San Francisco Marionettes had swam the Golden Gate Bridge demonstrating that synchronized swimmers were athletes as well, and I was inspired, maybe a bit jealous. Funny how seeds get planted.

I would try to switch my breathing from side to side but somehow it seemed disruptive. I'm not a fast swimmer, I just don't give up. One of the challenges of a swim like this is the barge schedule. I thought about that, and my movement through life. Around the backside of Alcatraz, I looked at the structures on the Island and wondered if inmates hadn't been told it was impossible to escape if more would have? What had I been told was impossible?

The current changed and I noticed that with each stroke I was seeing the same sign that read WARNING…. letting people know you could be imprisoned if you helped or concealed a prisoner. I began to feel nauseous. No matter how hard or long I stroked, the sign was still there. When I finally turned the eastern corner of the island the tide began to push me out towards the Golden Gate Bridge. I couldn't make it into the opening of the breakwater as the current was too strong and I was pushed past it. My friend picked me up under the bridge. He wrapped me in blankets and we headed back to the clubhouse. As I thawed out in a cool shower and later in a sauna, the feeling came creeping back into my limbs and then my body with a stinging effect. I drove home, had a bite to eat, and laid down to rest. When I awoke I called my friend, "I want to go again, I know I can make it. Will you pilot me tomorrow?". Bob, took a breath, "Let me check the barge schedule and the tide," he said, "it would have to be early, I'll call you back."

The following morning, as my toes touched the icy water around 4:30 am, the swim from the day before flashed before my eyes, the attempt, the fatigue, and the failure. I plunged in and started stroking into the dark water, again the splash of my stroke quieting my mind. Whenever fears would surface I'd pray, keep me safe, and I'd stroke through the fears attempting to disrupt my focus and peace of mind. I reached the island and could see the silhouettes of the structures as my head rotated sideways for air. It was slow going, slow and steady. I didn't feel the cold anymore, I kept moving. Around the backside, I once again saw the sign that indicated in large capital letters, bold-faced, WARNING, only this time the words were moving out of my peripheral vision more quickly. From time to time I caught glimpses of Bob, in the inflatable raft, knowing he was encouraging me onward. I was grateful for him. As I came around the last curve of the island and headed back towards the opening to the aquatic park I aimed East of the opening, remembering the pull of the current that took me out the Golden Gate the morning before. I could see the first light of morning as I stroked and kicked my way across the bay and into the opening. I slowed even more in the safety of the park's water. I wondered were they tears of joy, the warmth I felt on my cheeks against the icy water? My exhales deepened, I had made it in.

There isn't a day when I drive across the Golden Gate Bridge that I don't look out and say to myself, I swam that. I am often encouraged to plunge ahead with whatever my current challenge may be, knowing it too, will one day, be behind me.

Challenges are great teachers.

Don't give up.

CHAPTER THIRTY TWO (2005)
Mother

My mother was dying. She had an inoperable heart condition (calcium deposit on her aortic valve). Somewhere in the process of overseeing her care in the last year, it became important to me that she knew she was a great mother.

We had been through a lot together and the truth is the older I got the more I came to appreciate my mother. I could feel how hard she had tried, her unrelenting spirit, her many skills, and her dedication to my father.

Every time I was with her I would ask her, "Mom do you know you were a good mother?" She would reply with, "I tried hard", or " I sure loved your Dad", or "I did the best I could", but never quite able to simply accept what I was suggesting. Then one day I asked, as I always did, "Mom, do you know you were a good mother?" and she said, "I was, wasn't I?" I nearly yelled out loud, "YES." The next day I arrived and could hardly wait to hear her say it again. I walked in, gave her a hug, and then asked, confident in her reply, "Mom, do you know you were a good mother?" And she said, "I wasn't always late like you are."

My mother continued to teach me up until the very end of her life. She never let me relax into any version of "I've got this", which is such a good lesson. Life is a moment-to-moment experience unless I fall asleep to it.

Do you know you are amazing?

CHAPTER THIRTYTHREE (1994)
Small in a Big World

What I once started as an opportunity to stretch myself and heal from past wounds became something more. I swam out into the open ocean and what I felt as I looked back at the city awakening in the morning light was just how small I was in the big picture of things. Just a speck, a really small speck. My self-importance washed away as I felt the bigness of the world I was a small part of. I laughed, I cried, I trod water and looked around me as the sun was rising. Something deep inside of me was rising too. There was freedom in my smallness, in my inadequacy, in my efforts that failed over and over again. Surrendering wasn't giving up, it was giving way to something more wonderful than I could imagine. I put my head down and began to swim, stroking my way into the unknown of what lay ahead.

Sometimes a new view changes everything.

CHAPTER THIRTY FOUR (1970-1986)
The Day

The truth is I didn't actually qualify for doing much. For most of my educational years I was lost in addiction. Addicts know what I am talking about. Nothing mattered more than my addiction, not that I wanted to keep it in place, I just didn't know how to get beyond it.

There wasn't a day for 20 years that I didn't start out by saying, "This Is the Day", it just never was. I was always looking outside myself for inspiration, motivation. A new job, a new house, a Monday, the first day of Spring, Christmas. No matter what, it was never enough to stop the internal decay. Each new day added to my sense of failure.

Newness starts on
the inside

CHAPTER THIRTY FIVE (2005)

Burned with Anger

My mother had taken good care of all her belongings, and they were precious to her. When I was a child if something was broken, it was ruined, no matter how well my father repaired it, to her it had simply lost its value. When she was bedridden and there were caretakers in her house helping her she would lie in her room and hear things being dropped and or broken, and say, "I wonder what that was?" Eventually, after several months she would add, "Oh well, I guess it doesn't matter now."

She had hidden her jewelry behind pictures hanging on the walls, certain some of it was disappearing and "glued" down her most valued Lladro figurines. More than once I have reminded myself to recall her sense of helplessness should I find myself becoming attached to things, at the same time acutely aware of how fear sneaks in and takes up residence.

My mother also worried that someone would buy her house and cut down all the trees, which for 25 years she had lovingly cared for. I grappled with how as we age we hold on to the past. Somehow it is easier to see the struggles of life in others, and I watched them in my mother as I felt compassion for this powerhouse of a woman lying day after day unable to get up and move around, or control anything. A new meaning was added to the Christian hymn I sing, "I surrender all."

My eldest sister, who also loved her things, arrived shortly after my mother had gone to be with Jesus. She called me saying, "Some of mom's Lladros are missing," as she remembered counting them, "Did you happen to take them?" I shared with her the few I knew our mother had given as gifts, and thought I heard mistrust in her reply.

Arriving at the pool that morning I was angry, disappointed in how my sister was focusing on the "things" of our mother's life. I also felt accused rather than appreciated for how I had been there for her over the past few years. I swam hard, pounding the water with my strokes in the early dusk of morning, fuming as I went over our conversation again and again as I did a flip turn heading in the other direction while still stuck on the same conversation in my head.

 Once out of the pool I headed into the sauna, not that I needed to be any more heated. The last thing I remember was jumping off the top bench and slipping on the floor when I "awoke" and found myself lying by the door next to the sauna stove. I picked myself up and headed to the shower. As the water streamed from the shower I lifted my right arm and there was a large piece of something hanging between my arm and my side, like a giant wing. I put a towel around me and went to the front desk where I asked the person, "Can you look at my back?" I lowered the towel from my shoulders as he screamed quickly calling 911, asking me to wait there. I didn't feel anything. The paramedics came and took a look, they let me know I was severely burned and they were going to take me to the burn unit at the hospital for further treatment. I had been teaching a class called "One week without sugar, come meet God", for the past several weeks. I called my husband and asked him if he could cancel my class that morning and meet me at the hospital.

The paramedics talked with me in the ambulance asking me more questions and letting me know the reason I wasn't feeling any pain was due to being in shock. I remember being particularly present, kind, and polite. My desire to stay out of trouble runs deep. When my husband asked me, "What were you thinking right before you fell?" I realized how taken over with anger I was, "fuming" actually.

 After several days in the burn ward, I had surgery to remove all the dead skin and debris and apply pigskin so I could heal. When I awoke I was in excruciating pain and asked "why does it hurt so much, it feels like I am on fire?" They adjusted my pain medication, and when I opened my eyes someone was standing at the foot of my bed. It took me a moment to recognize my sister's son. I hadn't seen him in many years. I looked over to my side and saw my sister. I could still access the anger and frustration I had before the accident, but lying there I knew all there was to do was have compassion and love them both.

 Love has a way of asking more of us than we think we can give, and I have learned it is so love can give more to us than we think is possible.

 While it is always good to love the loveable, it's when we feel challenged to love that the real growth begins. Life is a love curriculum.

Anger is a great teacher when we stop, listen and ask what it wants or needs.

CHAPTER THIRTY SIX (2006)

On Love

Love is all-inclusive, it fulfills upon itself.

The only way to experience love is to BE loving. It starts with being. One way to distinguish being is through what we are thinking, speaking, believing, acting, and our attitude. If I am being irritated and someone is being loving towards me, I will experience irritation. To experience love I would keep my thoughts, words, actions, beliefs, and attitude on love.

When love is from the overflow (you know how loved you are) it is not depleted.

Love cannot be hurt or diminished. Love simply is.

You love to love, period. (there is no getting in loving)

Love is its own reward. (and you can't be looking for it)

If you are wanting more love, be more loving.

CHAPTER THIRTY SEVEN (1995)

This Moment

On another note, I had a dream about you last night. While the character was different I could tell it was inspired by our friendship.

In the dream, you lived with a sister. You and I had been in a class together and became close friends. The class was ending and I wanted to be sure to be able to stay in touch with you. I was trying to write down your contact info but kept hearing or getting the info wrong. I finally said, "Here", handing you my paper and pen, you wrote it down for me. I was thinking, I hope I can read your writing.

Some time passed and I wanted to reach out to you. I called the number you had written down and a girl answered. I asked if you were there and she asked me who was calling. I told her and heard her call out to you saying a friend from school was on the phone. I waited but you never got on the line. I awoke.

What I believe the dream meant is how important it is to leave all people knowing how much they mean to me. To be sure to let them know they are loved, as you never know if you are going to meet them again.

Do the people you love know how loved they are?

CHAPTER THIRTY EIGHT (2004)

Make a Mess

We weren't really allowed to make messes. Toys were picked up and games put back together when we were finished playing. Everything had its place, and that included us. Fun was scheduled, as were chores. We learned to clean, do dishes, cook, pull weeds, and make beds, really good beds too. Once they were made you didn't sit on them, that's not what beds were made for.

We also had the best birthday parties. My mother created circuses and fashion shows where the kids all walked a plank and modeled their too-big dress-up clothes in floppy high heels. Inevitably they would wander off the plank onto the grass and lose their balance, especially me as walking a straight line just wasn't my forte.

When my husband and I opened our first cafe it became clear to me that I was going to need to let go of my attempts to keep things just the way I liked them. I have learned to see others as a contribution rather than a liability.

While I appreciate order, I am closest to the people who have walked through life's messes with me.

It's the process that counts. Enjoy the journey, it may be messy.

CHAPTER THIRTY NINE (2018)

History

I am not very intelligent. While I am often in the midst of a conversation about the impact of smartphones I am grateful for their nearly instant source of information. When most kids were focusing on their education I was either swimming or trying to find or avoid food and all the events that included food. I excelled at people skills, keeping track of where others were and what they were doing. My internal chatter was always assessing my surroundings as if planning an escape route. I prided myself on being super observant, my survival depended on it. While my skills have served me well I have often felt on the outside, looking in.

An evening now snuggled up on the couch with my husband watching a documentary film, or historical drama feels like catching up on classroom hours long ago lost.

Let yourself invest in lifelong learning.

CHAPTER FORTY (1987)
A New View

A glass of water looked different. Like springtime; fresh, clean, and welcoming. After all those years of drinking water to ease purging, my appreciation grew for the little things, the simple things, often overlooked. The colors on a flower, the dew on a blade of grass, the salt on a saltine cracker were magical and happiness welled up inside of me just noticing them. I would say to people when sharing about recovery, "I'm recovering all the broken off parts of myself."

I came to see addicts, after working with many, as some of the most gifted, talented, and bright lights I had ever met. Addiction is an alternate life that is created to avoid being responsible for being all you are created to be.

Who were you
created to be?
What alternative have
you created?

CHAPTER FORTY ONE (2021)
Hawklike Love

I've been watching two baby red tail hawks who live in the most amazing nest high up in one of our palm trees. The mother works diligently to hunt and feed them. Yesterday she flew above me with a squirrel in her mouth and the joy of those babies, who are really quite big now, could be heard throughout the farm as she pulled off pieces and fed them. In the afternoon as the wind began to pick up, one of the babies fell from the nest and got caught in the dried fronds several feet below. The sound was deafening as the mother and baby communicated in their own language. This morning I found feathers on the ground below the palm, too many feathers to have a good ending. There was silence from what was left of the nest high above. I don't know the whole story, surely one baby didn't make it and became the victim of a ground animal foraging in the dark of night. But what of the other baby?

Families are like this too, at least mine was. I survived the attacks of those who forage, wounded but alive and now healed. One of my sisters is healing too. I hope that's the same story of the other baby hawk, somewhere, out there, healing. My other sister is no longer with us. I have a wind chime with some of her ashes in it. I picked up some of the hawk feathers and tied them together as I placed them near my wind chime.

I've found myself still listening for the calls of the mother hawk to her young. It's been a couple of days since I have heard anything. I miss them. I hadn't realized how their language had become a part of my day. I've been thinking about my mother bringing me food as I lay starving in that hospital bed over 54 years ago, as she carried in Mountain Dew and cheese curls. I see now that she just wanted me to eat and my life to get back to normal, whatever that was. If only it had been about the food. I suspect her hawk-like energy wouldn't let her see any deeper as I lay there in an emotional coma. Eat, was her one command as she drove back and forth to the hospital, arms laden with food, much like the mother hawk I had watched for weeks. We are designed to keep our young alive, it's a sign of sickness when we no longer do.

The deeper we know ourselves, the deeper is our capacity to know others intimately.

CHAPTER FORTY TWO (1978)

Mothers and Daughters

My husband had been away for several months and that time gave me an amazing opportunity to be strong, rise up in being responsible, and also get to know myself in new ways. Have you ever had that experience when something was needed from you and you didn't really think about whether or not you had what it took? It was simply yours to rise up into. I rose, not by myself but with the support of my farm crew, my family, and my inner guidance.

Motherhood is like that as well. You discover you are pregnant, you go through nine months of waiting and then there is the birthing process and suddenly there you are, a mother. Some little being is relying on you 24/7. While adapting yourself to all the changes in your own body, you have another little body, who is changing by the second, and they are yours to care for as well, you rise up.

I wish I could tell you that I rose up from the day my first child was born, but that simply wouldn't be the truth. I was still living with my addiction, my eating disorder through all of my children's births. I tried to be good, that was how I saw it. I tried to not eat or eat well, but the addiction was too far along and too big for me to face alone and I was still living in secrecy.

The normal fears a pregnant woman feels when they are healthy are magnified when they are not. My heart still goes out to all the women who find themselves carrying another human being while still struggling to care for themselves. It is a complicated situation.

My mother said once that she always loved being pregnant and took extra good care of herself. I could agree that I loved being pregnant. The thought of having a child to love inspired me, but I wouldn't say I took extra good care of myself unless you count swallowing a vitamin with a glass of milk right before I went to bed "extra". Which it was. While I worried about the health of my babies, they were all born naturally and healthy with birthing weights ranging between 7lbs 11 ounces and 7lbs 14 ounces. How does that happen? Again, it's hard for me not to acknowledge the miracle of life, the blessing of creation, and the presence of grace.

Once I had my children, caring for them came naturally to me. I love children, I love holding babies and I love watching children learn and grow. Taking care of myself was the part I struggled with. It was my middle child, my daughter, that I had the most challenge with. It wasn't her, it was me. I wanted a girl and was overjoyed when she was born. I hadn't received any prenatal care and had just walked out of an abusive relationship, we were both addicts.
I was working as a cocktail waitress in the pub of a local inn. I share this, partly to give hope to those who might find themselves in a similar situation or seeking forgiveness for a past one.

One night after work we were all sitting around listening to a band when I had the desire for a coca-cola. I never drank coke and had the thought that soon I was going into labor. I don't know what the connection was, it's just the way it happened. I asked a good friend if he could take me to the hospital. He looked in the yellow pages and found a hospital nearby, Magee's Women's Hospital in Pittsburgh, Pennsylvania. I remember thinking it sounded like a friendly hospital. My best friends took care of my 2-year-old son and we left.

A heavy-set nurse greeted us and told me she would have the doctor check me and then send me on my way home (I remember wondering just where home was). She simply didn't believe me when I said I was going to have a baby, you see, I didn't look pregnant. I had actually lost weight, not gained any. The doctor came in and checked me and said with a surprise, "She is right and she is going to have her baby really soon."

They rushed me into Labor and Delivery and within the hour my baby girl was born.
My friend ordered pizza for the staff and they put me in a room. I'm actually not sure how that delivery was paid for, I didn't have insurance or the money, but I did name my little girl after the hospital.

Turns out that little girl had an independent spirit in her. When I failed to rock her cradle she figured out how to rock it herself. Now, that isn't something I am proud of and yet somehow we seem to get what we need. She needed that spirit in her and I needed her to have it. Call it whatever you want, I call it God's grace. That same little girl is the one who questioned me when I came out of the bathroom seven-plus years later and she is the one who led me back to God's love and into recovery.

So wherever you are when Mother's Day is celebrated, whatever the condition of your mothering, no matter how difficult or wonderful it may seem to be responsible for the life of another little human being, please know that none of us already have what it takes. We all need the grace that comes from a Father who loves us long before we love ourselves, to rise up and embrace what it is to be a mother.

My daughter has always questioned if she has anything special to offer. I pray she now knows that there is nothing about her that isn't special.

Grace is a gift, freely given.

Social Media

What if social media led everyone to the foot of Jesus…. or to love?
What would they see
What would they read
What would they experience
And if your activity was tracked
What offers would be brought into your feed?
What ads would you see?

Our lives leave a trail.
Where is yours leading?

Shift your input and
it shifts your output.

CHAPTER FORTY FOUR (1969)

Loss

My Wedding night

I don't remember anything except soft pretzels and aebleskivers, both of which I wanted but was afraid to eat. Addiction steals memorable moments.

Leave behind your willingness to just survive so you can thrive.

Trading Shoelaces

I was in a crowded room when I noticed a man across the room looking directly at me. As he walked toward me I saw that he was wearing jogging shorts and white athletic socks with rather ragged running shoes. His hair was dark and curly and his skin a beautiful black. He walked right up to me saying, "I've been looking for you." I was caught a bit off guard as I replied, "You have?" "Yes," he said as he put his hands in his pockets as if looking for something. He glanced up and asked, "How are you going to mark our meeting?" I wasn't quite sure what he meant, as he continued to search. Then, as if he had an idea, he bent down and began to untie one of his shoelaces. "I know", he remarked, "Let's trade shoelaces." I looked down at my fairly new red boots and thought to myself, his shoelaces aren't as nice as mine, but oh well, I can trade and then always get a new one to replace it later. I undid one of my laces as he handed me his.

Then I awoke.
Laying there I realized he was Jesus.

> Love always has a way of bringing our shortcomings to the surface and gently gives us the opportunity to learn more about loving well.

CHAPTER FORTY SIX (2020)

Rescued

A small bird built a nest in a hanging plant in the front courtyard. I kept my eye on it while the mother was laying her eggs, five in total in such a tiny nest. I began to worry that the nest would be too small for five baby birds. Lifting the plant down one day I saw all five eggs had hatched and those little birds were no bigger than one joint on my baby finger.

Walking out my bedroom door one morning, with our dog Bella, my eye caught something small laying on the patio walkway. I immediately distracted Bella, zeroed in on the tiny newborn bird laying there, and quickly swooped down and put it in the palm of my hand, and lifted it back into the nest above my head.

Later in church that morning while singing a worship song tears began to roll down my cheeks. I realized that the same way I DIDN'T think but quickly acted and rescued that little bird is the same way God rescues us. He is right there, waiting for us to turn towards Him and when we do he swoops in and gently puts us back where we belong, in his care. I can see that I overthink it sometimes, that there are just as many potential emergency situations with people in my life as there were with that little bird.

I'm going to start swooping them up and pointing them towards home. Love always wins.

Gratitude is the knowledge of having received and the willingness to give in return.

CHAPTER FORTY SEVEN (1972)

Miracles

The flight crew started talking about renting a ski boat on our layover and going water skiing. I love water sports. Tahoe was beautiful and warm and the water was crisp, my favorite combination. I didn't bring a bathing suit on the trip but the flight engineer offered to take me shopping. I don't remember much except I loved the yellow suit we found, and while I was sensitive about the price tag he said he wanted to pay for it. I liked it enough to push past my discomfort in receiving the gift. Leaving Chicago a few days earlier we had all become quick friends. It wasn't every crew that enjoyed each other as this one did.

On the water, we took turns skiing. I was excited and a bit nervous waiting for my turn. I floated in the water skis while the boat started picking up speed, and soon I was up! The wind, the water, the sound of the spray, and the faces of my new friends encouraged me on, crisscrossing the wake added an extra thrill. Then suddenly the slack in the tow rope drew taut and I fell forward with a jerk. I let go of the rope and while underwater realized that I hadn't even thought about my new upper denture, but it was gone. I thought, there is no way I am coming up without my teeth, I'd rather die first. I silently called out God PLEASE, when I opened my eyes I saw them floating down in front of me heading for the bottom and out of sight. I reached out, grabbed them, put them in my mouth, and popped up to the surface just as the boat had circled around to pick me up. I took a deep breath and was flooded with gratitude as they pulled me in.

Now I don't know the chances of that happening, but I've tried in a pool, no boat, no speed, to see how fast they sink and it's fast enough that I call what happened a miracle. Whenever I question God I remember this and my experience always outweighs my doubt.

I also learned to always close my mouth when doing anything that could jar them loose again.

See, I think it would have been easy for me to surface and call it a coincidence, or luck, but in doing so I would have diminished how cared for I was.

Take a breath and
expand your chest,
open your heart
and feel the bless-
ing that belongs in
your story.

CHAPTER FORTY EIGHT (1990)
Getting Closer

I was visiting my parents pretty early into recovery, which quite frankly stretched everyone. It isn't easy when your perceptions of someone get confronted as they become more transparent. You are left to deal with those perceptions and sometimes question just where you were when they were going through all their challenges.

I think it was like that for my father.

He was a quiet man and must have been processing his questions before he spoke saying, "Sweetie, so you were dealing with the eating disorder while you were pregnant with your children?" I looked up, a bit surprised as my parents had never really talked with me about my experience, and replied, "yes." He said with a shaky voice, "That must have been very difficult for you." My mother yelled out from the kitchen where she was making muffins, "What are you two saying?" My father called back, "She is sharing that she was dealing with her food issue while she was pregnant." My mother responded, "Oh, I always took good care of myself when I was pregnant with you girls." My father expressed his frustration when he said, "Didn't you hear what she said?" It was difficult for her". I spoke directly to my father saying, "I was so afraid that my babies would be born with something wrong". There were tears running down my cheeks. He sunk deeper into his chair and said, "When I was in the war we would all gather for breakfast and I would look around the table at the other men, the air raid alarm would go off and we would take off." He was sobbing now, my mother yelled out again, "Your father can't handle this." He went on, "We would come back from our mission and gather for the evening meal and I would look around at the empty chairs. I told myself I would never get that close to anyone ever again." He got up and walked out the back door. I went after him as I heard my mother yelling, "This isn't good for him, it's too much."

My father had never talked about the war. He wore a piece of shrapnel in his arm and only a few times did I hear him wince when it got bumped too hard. He flew PBY seaplanes in World War II used for bombing and for rescue. He went on later in his Naval career to teach aviation before retiring and having a second career as a high school mathematics teacher. He was one of four sons and a sister born in Bisbee, Arizona. His mother ran a boarding house for copper miners after his father was killed in a mining accident that was always reported as suspicious. His father had been blackballed as he fought on behalf of the miners for more safety in the mines. My father once told me that he was waiting in the yard when he was 12 years old for his dad to come home from work, on the day he was killed. He ran to the desert to grieve alone and it was there he first had a direct experience of God. Years later, when I sat next to my father as he was dying I questioned him about life, not wanting the wisdom I knew he had to die with him. He said his only regret was he didn't share more of his faith with his girls.

As he lay there in the hospital bed staring up at the acoustic ceiling panels, I couldn't imagine what he was seeing, so I asked, "Daddy what are you thinking about?"

He quietly said, "Love."

Reach out and connect with someone you have closed your heart to.

CHAPTER FORTY NINE (2016)

Joy

I became aware that fear was sneaking into my life, beginning to rob me of some of my joy. I'm pretty good at confronting it however I found myself saying, "it doesn't really matter," or "it could be so much worse," thinking I was diminishing the power fear can have. However, I recognized I was actually denying my unwillingness to address it.

I wrote a letter to my ex-husband asking if it would be okay for us to dance together at our son's wedding. I also asked if I would be able to come and see him if he was dying before I did. I don't know why questions like this arise, they just do.

He wrote back that he would ask his wife about the dance and he couldn't imagine that either one of us would die in a vacuum, as we shared a son, and he would surely know what was happening in either of our worlds, and he would be sure that he knew that I was welcome to come and see him.

As the wedding drew near, he wrote again saying he didn't think the dance would be possible as it would be too uncomfortable for his wife. I could feel the letting go happening inside of me. I think it's like that with long-held hopes, childhood dreams, or even cultural expectations that we might not even have chosen yet we live with them, and maybe there is some pain wanting to be soothed, some sorrow still unexpressed seeking freedom.

The wedding was small and beautiful, simple and elegant. By the time there was some dancing I was already snuggled into the bed with a grandchild needing some comforting and rest, in the studio off the veranda where the dancing was taking place. I hadn't thought much of the missed opportunity as I lay there listening to the music while feeling the warmth of a sleeping child. The door opened and someone came in to use the bathroom, on their way out I opened my eyes and I saw the image of a man and child in the darkened room. Only moments after I felt someone kiss me gently on the cheek. It took me a while before I realized that it was the father of my youngest son whose wedding it was.

I've often thought of the kindness of his action, no words were spoken and yet my desire for the opportunity to dance was more than fulfilled.

God works in miraculous ways to heal the broken hearted.

Thin-Skinned

It doesn't take much to cause a bruise or broken skin lately. I sometimes look down only to find blood dripping down my leg after what seems like the slightest of scrapes against almost anything. I remember my mother sharing about the same thing as she was still pruning trees in her front yard at nearly 80 years old. I used to feel her skin as she lay bedridden near the end of her life slowly running out of oxygen and it felt so thin and silky to my touch. My skin feels more like hers every day. I am so grateful I'm not running out of oxygen as I remember to give thanks for each breath. I often say yes quietly to myself on my inhale and thank you as I exhale. It is such a good reminder of the fragility of life and the blessing of each breath, so freely given and sometimes so quickly taken away. As my skin grows thinner my spirit grows more durable. What used to wreck me internally, literally has me sitting on the floor hugging my knees as I weep, barely scratching the surface of my peaceful center now. Thank goodness for those people who challenged me and thus taught me to love myself and others.

My life is not about me, but I am about my life.

As author Margery Williams has shared with us all, I am in the becoming years of life. It's taken a long time. Looking back is not the same as an awakening "in it". I appreciate that. For those of you who are still "in it" be patient and kind with yourselves. The day will come when you may look back and wish you had done more with your youth, appreciated who you were, and will wonder what if? Unless you take this moment, this day, and live it full out, not foolishly but lovingly.

The snares of distraction are all around us and unless we learn to use them as beacons steering us towards love and away from fear it is quite easy to be misguided. Keep looking up, surround yourself with those who inspire and encourage you, pay attention to all that you put in yourself; your food, your music, your images, your words, they are the nourishment you will depend on. I spent way too many years living my life by observing those around me and trying to take direction from their choices. Make your own choices and trust those, because fitting in isn't living.

There is a small quiet and powerful voice in each of us, live to hear it. That is a different life than the one which drowns out that eternal wisdom. Seek stillness, you will actually accomplish much more than you imagine. Learn to listen, it is one of the most loving acts you can do and it requires very little action. It is much more difficult to do nothing than we might think. If you find yourself fixing or changing others it's a good indication that there is work for you to do within yourself.

The world shows up in our viewfinder, keep yours clean and clear. What is popular today will be ridiculous tomorrow. Seek what is true and will always be true, be wary of stories. I say that as I am sharing my story with you, don't get caught up in my story either, listen for what rings true for you, trust that. My guiding light has always been Jesus. I have run into more folks who struggle with him than agree. I actually think that is good medicine for me; to question the common opinion and seek my own experience. Relationships are personal, they require that you give of yourself and interact with another who is also giving of themselves. Once that happens with Jesus, you are never the same again, and sometimes that starts with you disagreeing with Him. I don't think He minds. Seeking agreement may lead to following a crowd. He said, "Follow me", and that's a personal invitation. Why not see where it goes?

Who or what are you following?

CHAPTER FIFTY TWO (2005)
Cafe Gratitude

Standing on the opposite side of the street in the Mission District of San Francisco, looking at the lit cafe the night before we opened our doors, I realized I had come full circle.

We were creating an opportunity for people to celebrate with those they love without feeling guilty about what they ate or drank. They would be able to toast one another with a healthy green drink served in a beautiful wine glass and stay present rather than slowly numbing themselves. Our handful of new employees was taking on practicing being grateful no matter what the circumstances of their lives were and being acknowledged as the leaders they had perhaps never known themselves as. People would be coming and in and just ordering a drink or something to eat affirming the best of who they are.

It was my way of giving away what I had been given.

There is always something to be grateful for.

ACKNOWLEDGEMENTS

I Am Grateful For You

As I think about you, all of you who have so generously contributed to this book, my heart is filled with gratitude. From the encouragement you gave me to the final editing, I have felt your support and love. In the early days, it was my children who gave me the courage to keep on going, and their belief in me made my journey meaningful. Matthew, Molly, and Cary, I love and thank you. In the later years, it was my husband who taught me to love no matter what, for which I am grateful. Some of my most powerful teachers have been those who found it difficult to love or forgive me. Ultimately you helped make me a better person. Bianca Olthoff, your encouragement fueled me whenever I got caught in thinking my story didn't matter. Kim McManus, your words always give my journey validity and support me in keeping faith in a loving Jesus. I suspect as Bob Goff says, we all have at least one book in us, our task is to let it out. Thank you for your enthusiasm. Joanna Waterfall and Elyse Snipes, partnering with you two was fun and enlightening. Christyl and Justin Brown, thank you for all those years ago picking me up and dusting me off, your love is healing. Jyoti and Russell, for all the hours of sitting together and sharing dreams and visions that came to life. Jennifer Rosenthal, you are the perfect editor. You made sure each word mattered, and what an honor it was to work with you. Jon Marro, thank you for your guidance, artistic skill, and friendship. I also give thanks for the ongoing guidance of that still small voice that restored my trust and never fails to lead to love. Lastly, thank you to my fifteen grandchildren, it is through you that I glimpse a better future.

While gratitude may start with all there is to give thanks for, it is my experience that if we keep on practicing, one day we no longer look for reasons to be grateful, we simply are unreasonably grateful and live in grace by choice.

Thank you all,
Love,
Terces

ABOUT THE AUTHOR

How Loved You Are

Terces Engelhart wants to make sure people don't miss, how loved they are. Her love and acceptance are welcoming and her joy is infectious. Her journey from sexual abuse to twenty years of an eating disorder empowers her sharing real-life experiences and her intimate relationship with Jesus, which led to her healing, is inspiring. She enjoys sharing with others through her podcast Unreasonably Grateful and when not speaking publically, she lives with her husband, Matthew in the Northwest on their regenerative farm. She and her husband are the founders of Cafe Gratitude and Gracias Madre, plant-based restaurants. Together they have five grown children and fifteen grandchildren.

Gratitude is a place we come from, not get to.

Lightning Source UK Ltd.
Milton Keynes UK
UKHW020800170922
408977UK00006B/252